my NEW BOOK

THE UPCOMING MESSAGE
THAT WILL CHANGE THE WORLD!

BY

CATHY FYOCK
The Business Book Strategist

&

EVERETT O'KEEFE
Founder, Ignite Press

IGNITE
PRESS
Fresno, CA

Published in the United States by
Ignite Press
5070 N. Sixth St. #189
Fresno, CA 93710
www.IgnitePress.us

ISBN: 979-8-9851961-0-8

For bulk purchase and for booking, contact:

Cathy Fyock
Cathy@CathyFyock.com

Library of Congress Control Number: 2021950010

Cover design by Randy Martin & Everett O'Keefe
Edited by Charlie Wormhoudt
Interior design by Amit Dey

ADVANCE PRAISE FOR
MY NEW BOOK

"I only wish I had this to read beside the pond."

— Henry David Thoreau

"A work of art!"

— Leonardo Da Vinci

"Here is a lever to move the world!"

— Archimedes

"This is a book to bring about the best of times!"

— Charles Dickens

"A book of great gravity!"

— Sir Isaac Newton

"If you are deciding which way to go, you'll want this book!"

— Robert Frost

"You won't be able to throw this one back!"

— Loren Eiseley

TABLE OF CONTENTS

INTRODUCTION

If you've been dreaming of writing your first (or next) book, this workbook is designed for you. In the pages ahead, you will capture the ideas for your upcoming book with the help of insightful questions and prompts in a structured format. In fact, this workbook will provide you with all the tools you need to outline your book and create the strategic direction to see it finished!

We have left you space to write your answers directly in this book. Nonetheless, feel free to use a separate notebook, Google Doc, or other tool to keep your content organized. Whatever you do, make sure to keep all of your content in one place. This will help keep you organized and will also help prevent the loss of key information or ideas.

Feel free to skip around and complete sections as you are inspired. This workbook is a tool for your inspiration and organization. Don't be a slave to the tool. Put it to work in the way that serves you best.

Supplies and Resources:

- Sticky notes: some exercises will encourage the use of sticky notes. Make sure to have a full pad handy!

- Colored pencils or pens: some people love to use a special pen or colors. Others could care less. Use whatever works best for you.

There are two great companion pieces for this book:

- *On Your Mark: From First Word to First Draft in Six Weeks* by Cathy Fyock.

  You have a book inside you, but how do you get it out? This book offers tips for identifying obstacles, making a game plan, creating momentum, and finishing your draft.

- *The Power of the Published: How Rapidly Authoring a Book Can Ignite Your Business and Your Life* by Everett O'Keefe

  Through real-life examples, this book shows the many ways a book can impact a brand or organization. The second half of the book walks authors through the pros and cons of traditional, self-, and hybrid publishing.

If you have questions or would like to discuss additional services from Cathy Fyock, The Business Book Strategist, contact Cathy at 502-445-6539 or Cathy@CathyFyock.com.

When you want to discuss publishing options and Amazon bestseller campaigns, you may take advantage of a complimentary book consultation with Everett O'Keefe. Just visit IgnitePress.us to arrange a meeting.

PLANNING YOUR SUCCESS

Writing a book isn't about putting a lot of words on pages. It requires a game plan that starts with the strategic alignment of your book to your purpose. The exercises and worksheets provided here will help you flesh out the plan you'll need to use to build your book. We'll start with the purpose for your book, the thesis, the targeted reader, and the content outline.

While we start here, you don't need to work through the book sequentially. Feel free to jump around and follow your energy. Remember that building your book is a huge task, and you want to create small wins in order to build your confidence and momentum, which will lead to flow!

Where there are word prompts, I suggest that you set the timer for a short amount of time to complete the exercise. You can always come back and add to your thoughts. By having a set period of time to work you'll begin to write first and edit second—these are two distinct brain functions and if you try to edit as you creatively write you'll burn yourself out!

While these exercises are intended for you to work through on your own, if you'd like a guide to help you, please call Cathy at Cathy@CathyFyock.com to discuss your project.

The Why of Your Book

Why are you writing your book? Put a check mark next to the reasons that apply to you, and add your own if you like.

- ❏ Expert positioning
- ❏ Speaking opportunities
- ❏ Media attention
- ❏ Industry recognition
- ❏ Elite status
- ❏ Elimination of competition
- ❏ Greater customer retention
- ❏ Durable marketing tool
- ❏ Social proof
- ❏ Persuasion of clients
- ❏ Increase fees
- ❏ Higher-value clients
- ❏ Profitable opportunities
- ❏ Business card
- ❏ Revenue stream
- ❏ Foundation for online course
- ❏ Build confidence

Other reasons or benefits:

Your Book and Your Business

How will your book interface with your business?

Examples:

- Pipeline for future business opportunities
- Coaching or training class curriculum
- Preview your values, philosophies, approaches, processes
- Reinforcement for other forms of learning (webinar, class-room training)
- Thank you or give-away
- Evidence of expertise

Your Life as a Published Author

Write a short story about your life as a published author. What are you doing? How is your business growing? What is the media saying about you? Include as many details as you can.

🖋 Positioning Statement

Write your professional positioning statement:

Example: My name is Cathy Fyock, and I work with professionals and thought leaders who want to write a book as a business growth strategy.

My name is _____ and I

work with (who?) _____

_____

_____

_____

_____

so that they can (do what?) _____

_____

_____

_____

_____ .

Thesis Statement

Write your thesis statement. What is your book about? What is the book's theme or message?

You'll ultimately want a very short (30-second commercial) version, a short summary, and a longer summary for the book's back cover, for Amazon, and for your collateral materials.

Target Market

Write down the words that describe your ideal client / target reader. Consider job titles, demographics, and psychographics (how do they feel about your topic?). Where are they on their journey relative to your thesis?

A Letter to Your Reader

Write a letter to your reader. What would you like to say? What outcomes would you like to see for them?

A Letter from Your Reader

Write a letter from your reader to *you*. Be imaginative. What do you hope your reader would say to you?

A Story About Your Reader

Write a story about your reader. What does your reader do after reading your book? How is your reader's life impacted or changed? Be creative. Use dialogue if you want!

Your Reviews

☆ ☆ ☆ ☆ ☆

Write at least five reviews of your book from readers who loved it. Describe how the book impacted each reader. What was each reader's ROI (return on investment)? How did your book help each reader?

Organizing Thoughts and Chapters

Write a list of questions that your reader has about your thesis. After creating a list here, rewrite each question on its own sticky note.

Write a list of key stories (from your experience, from your clients, or from history/literature) that relate to your thesis. After creating your list here, rewrite each story (keywords) on its own sticky note.

Write a list of data points, quotes, illustrations, or models that relate to your thesis. After creating your list here, write each item on a sticky note (one item per sticky note).

Exercise: Organize your sticky notes into chapters. You may group them here in this book, or you may want to post them on a wall in your office or workspace.

Chapter 1

Chapter 2

Chapter 3

Chapter 4

Chapter 5

Chapter 6

Chapter 7

Chapter 8

Chapter 9

Chapter 10

Use additional pages if you want to include more chapters. There is no ideal number of chapters in a book. Use the following pages to flesh out details for each chapter.

Chapter 1

Chapter 2

Chapter 3

Chapter 4

Chapter 5

Chapter 6

Chapter 7

Chapter 8

Chapter 9

Chapter 10

Pick one of the thesis-related questions from your targeted readers, and write a short (500–700 word) blog post answering that question.

Write a story that connects to your thesis. It may begin with, "Once upon a time . . ."

Prompts

What follows are a series of prompts that are intended to spur your thinking about your message. Look at the words or images, relate those words or images to your message, and GO. There are no right or wrong answers—just see where the prompts take you. Set your timer for two, five, or ten minutes, but don't give yourself unlimited time. Remember that you only want to *write* and that these exercises do not involve *editing*.

Prompt #1: Three things you either must do or must not do.

Prompt #2: Three secrets.

Prompt #3: Three mistakes you have made.

Prompt #4: Three steps to success.

Prompt #5:

Prompt #6:

Prompt #7:

Prompt #8:

Prompt #9:

Prompt #10:

Prompt #11:

Overcoming Obstacles (Dealing with the Negative Voice)

We all have a "negative voice" (what Cathy likes to call The B!%$#) inside our heads. What does your negative voice say to you?

What person's voice do you hear when the negative voice speaks? A critical parent? A demanding teacher? Your spouse?

Write a letter to your negative voice (feel free to begin, "Dear B!%$#"). What do you want to tell your negative voice? Be emphatic! Be emotional! Tell it off!! Do you need to thank your negative voice?

About the Author

Write a list of your most important accomplishments or credentials that relate to this book's thesis.

Write a list of all the ways in which you serve your clients (be specific about speaking, consulting, coaching, etc.).

Write a list of fun facts that you'd be willing to share with your readers. Include hobbies, family, favorite places or things, etc.

Now write your "About the Author" using one or two data points from each list.

Acknowledgements

Create a list of people who have helped you with your book. What did each contribute?

Consider the following:

Family

Colleagues

Friends

Publisher

Editor

Book coach

Editorial board / beta readers

Mentor

Mastermind

Contact the Author

Let your readers know how they can reach you, and what things you'd love to discuss with them (consulting, speaking, coaching, etc.).

Monthly Blog Posts

Write down one topic for each month, making sure each topic relates to your thesis. *Example: January = new beginnings.*

- ➤ January

- ➤ February

- ➤ March

- ➤ April

- ➤ May

- ➤ June

- ➤ July

- ➤ August

- ➤ September

- ➤ October

- ➤ November

- ➤ December

On the following pages write one short blog post (350–750 words) for each month's theme. Use additional pages or your computer if needed.

January Blog Post (350–750 words):

February Blog Post (350–750 words):

March Blog Post (350–750 words):

April Blog Post (350–750 words):

May Blog Post (350–750 words):

June Blog Post (350–750 words):

July Blog Post (350–750 words):

August Blog Post (350–750 words):

September Blog Post (350–750 words):

October Blog Post (350–750 words):

November Blog Post (350–750 words):

December Blog Post (350–750 words):

Testimonials

Create a wish list of people who would give credibility to your book, including friends, colleagues, and those you don't know (yet).

THE GREAT DILEMMA: TRADITIONAL VS. SELF-PUBLISHING

By

Everett O'Keefe

As an author, you are going to be faced with a decision once you finish writing: Should you attempt to secure a traditional publishing contract for your book, or should you wade into the complexities of self-publishing in order to get your book out to the world?

Traditional Publishing

Traditional publishing has its attractions. First, most traditional companies will handle all the technical details associated with publishing. The publisher will provide editing, interior layout, and cover development. They will arrange publishing and (perhaps) distribution, along with other services.

While these are great benefits, many authors are most attracted to the idea of traditional publishing because of other expectations. There is the expectation that the publishing company will pay them a substantial advance for the privilege of publishing their book. Authors also often expect that the publisher will arrange for publicity and marketing...and see to it that their books populate the shelves at local bookstores.

Red Light

Unfortunately, the reality of traditional publishing may be somewhat different. First, traditional publishing houses are taking on fewer and fewer projects each year, and the size of advances are shrinking for all but the most established personalities. What's more, most houses are not interested in new authors unless they already have a huge following and established track record in moving merchandise. This is what I call the Red Light of Traditional Publishing.

Did you know that the first Harry Potter book was initially rejected by multiple publishing agents and approximately a dozen publishers? J. K. Rowling continued to push her book, and it was finally accepted by Bloomsbury (who only paid her a £1,500 advance, by the way!). Somewhere along the line, someone told her "not to quit her day job."

In fact, rejection is a common theme for many successful writers. Let's take a look:

- Stephen King's *Carrie*, rejected 30 times
- *The Lord of the Flies* by William Golding, rejected 20 times
- John le Carré's *The Spy Who Came in from the Cold*, rejected with the admonition that he "hasn't got any future"
- *Gone with the Wind* by Margaret Mitchell, rejected 38 times
- *The Diary of a Young Girl* by Anne Frank, rejected 15 times
- Louisa May Alcott (*Little Women*) was told teaching would be better
- *Dune* by Frank Herbert, 23 rejections
- *Dubliners* by James Joyce, 22 rejections

- 121 rejections for Robert Pirsig and his *Zen and the Art of Motorcycle Maintenance*!

Fortunately, these authors ultimately persevered to get their work published. Are you up for such a battle?

Time

What's more, you need to know that there are some downsides to traditional publishing. For all the wonderful things that publishers do, the traditional process takes time...lots of time. First, you must successfully attract a publishing agent who both sees your vision and has relationships with publishers that publish your type of book. This takes time to happen. Then, the agent must shop the book to find the appropriate publisher. This takes time as well. Finally, if the agent is successful in finding a publisher to accept the project, the actual publishing process will often take 12–18 months (or more).

Do you have years to wait to put your book to work for you? Many authors do not. If you go the traditional publishing route, just plan that it may take two or even three years to see your book in print.

Other Challenges

In addition, many traditional publishers fail to provide the publicity and marketing that authors crave. Instead, even traditionally published authors find themselves forced to arrange their own publicity and marketing services, often at great expense.

There is also the issue of rights. Publishers often demand control of the book content as well as how that content is used in other publications and media. Authors who land a publishing contract often find they have their hands tied. Many are unable to repurpose their content, give books away, sell books "back of room," or create derivative works without the blessing (and financial involvement) of their publisher.

Royalties are a challenge too. Most publishers pay authors between 8% and 20% on the sale of a book, and this is after deductions for printing, marketing, and distribution. For this reason, even many famous authors make very little on their books and must make their money in other ways (movie rights, speaking fees, consulting, etc.).

Even acquiring and using "author copies" can be problematic. Authors are typically unable to acquire their own books at cost. Although they do receive a discount, they may still pay two to four times the actual printing cost of the book.

None of this is to say that traditional publishing is bad. It can be great for the *right author* and with the *correct contract*. Authors with a huge following and market exposure can benefit greatly from such publishing. And few can argue with the *cachet* that comes from being published by one of the large publishing houses. Traditional publishing can be an excellent option in the right circumstances. Authors simply need to understand the tradeoffs that come with this option.

Self-Publishing

I am a huge fan of self-publishing. In fact, that is how I started in the publishing world and how I learned many (often difficult) lessons. Self-publishing has tremendous advantages. Of course, it has its own tradeoffs, too.

Speed to Market

While traditional publishing of a book can take years, self-publishing may take months. I wrote and published my first book in under 30 days. It wasn't any good (and I burned a lot of midnight oil), but I did it! Self-publishing works at your speed...at least in part. If you choose to employ an editor, layout artist, or cover artist, they will take some time. But generally you can move much more quickly than a large publishing house; certainly you can see your book in print in months instead of years.

Green Light

Unlike in traditional publishing, there is no one to tell you "no." You alone decide if your book will be published. This is both good and bad! It is good because you probably know best how you will use your book and whether it will be effective for you. It is bad because there is no one to keep you from publishing a poorly written or designed book. As such, it is very possible for you to place a powerful and useful message in a package that is completely unprofessional and unreadable. But at least no one can keep you from publishing your book.

Control

You have complete control in self-publishing. You can determine your book's length, style, voice, etc. You can select your title, cover, interior design, artwork, and more. You get to determine your publishing, distribution, and marketing. Of course, this means you also *must* determine these things. Much like the "green light" scenario described above, this is both good and bad. Many authors find that they desire and enjoy creative control...to a point. When they reach that point, they then crave the input and expertise of professionals in these areas.

Printing

This is an area where self-publishing absolutely shines. If you self-publish, you can get your books at cost, and you have the freedom to print your books anywhere and any way you like.

One great option is Print-on-Demand (POD) printing. I call this the eighth wonder of the world for authors. With POD, Amazon does not stock a supply of your books. Instead, they house your book *files*. When someone orders your book, they print that one copy and ship it, usually within 24 hours! It really is a modern-day miracle.

As an author, you can take advantage of this technology to get copies of your book for your own use, too. You can simply order the number of author copies you need whenever you need them. There is no minimum print run, and the per-copy price is very affordable, often under $3 a book. This means you can order one or 500 books, and you can have them drop shipped wherever you like. This is especially good if you are traveling to a speaking engagement or trade show. Your books can meet you there!

You also have the freedom to do whatever you like with these copies; you can give them away to clients or prospects, sell them, bundle them in with speaking contracts, etc. You are your own publisher, so do what you like!

The Best of Both Worlds

While self-publishing has numerous advantages, there is one serious disadvantage. You can see it in the very term: self-publishing. Self-publishing in the purest sense relies upon you to carry out the entire publishing process. Not only do you have to create the manuscript, but you have to get it edited, find and supervise a professional interior layout artist, create or source a professional cover, and complete the myriad steps to make your book available for printing, distribution, and marketing. These steps include (among others) keyword research, category research, pricing, creation of the book description, ISBN registration, proofing, graphic configuration, and much, much more. The details are many, and getting even one of them wrong can cause frustration and embarrassment.

For this reason, there is a third type of publishing: hybrid publishing. Hybrid publishing allows you to enjoy all of the advantages of self-publishing without having to do all the work! By engaging with what is called a "hybrid publisher," you get to remove the "self" from the majority of the post-writing work. Rather than having to find a way to complete all phases of manuscript preparation, artwork development, publishing, distribution, and launch, you engage with a company that is experienced in all aspects of the process, and it completes these tasks for you.

These companies are called hybrid because they handle all the details and work of publishing your book like a traditional publisher, but you typically retain some or all the rights to your content and receive higher royalties like in self-publishing.

A hybrid publishing company should be able to handle all or nearly all aspects of bringing your book to market. Some will work with you to develop your initial book concept and guide you along the road to writing your manuscript. Others will only work with you when your manuscript is complete. Some will provide a "soup-to-nuts" approach, providing all the services needed to publish your book. Such companies may provide copy or line editing, interior layout, cover design, publishing, and even book launch services. Others are more limited in their offerings, focusing solely on placing your book for sale at various online outlets. Unlike traditional publishers, many hybrid publishers do not make money from book sales. All royalties flow directly to you. There is no middleman between you and your sales. As a result, many hybrid publishers operate on a fee-for-service basis.

Some hybrid publishers, however, operate a bit more like traditional publishers. Although they take a fee upfront, they also take a portion of sales. They may also apply a markup for author copies. The same paperback that might cost you $3 otherwise may be made available to you for $5 instead. While I have no objection to this model if this is properly disclosed, this type of hybrid publisher takes away some of the best advantages to self-publishing—in this case, higher royalties and lower cost of author copies.

A word of caution: If you hire a hybrid publishing company, determine in advance two things. First, will you own all of the rights to your content? Second, will you have an easy and affordable way to exercise those rights? Let me explain.

Some hybrid publishing companies take the approach of traditional publishers where they have you sign over all or part of the rights to your book and/or brand. They may demand exclusive rights to distribution, force you to buy author copies through them (at a marked-up cost), or otherwise limit (or eliminate) your ability to take your content and publish it elsewhere. This may be completely understandable in the case of a traditional publisher who has perhaps paid you a sizeable advance in exchange for these rights. In my opinion, this is not acceptable in the case of a hybrid publisher that you have paid to publish your book! If a company pays you to buy the rights to your intellectual property, that's fine. But you should never have to sacrifice your intellectual property rights without proper compensation.

Even if a company makes it clear that you own all the rights to your content, the company may make it expensive or difficult to exercise these rights. For instance, the company may charge a substantial fee to provide you with the source files for your book. It may charge a hefty change fee if you want to make even a small change to your online book description or alter the price of your Kindle ebook. While it is completely understandable for a company to charge a reasonable fee because of labor costs it incurs to make changes to a book, some companies seem to put charges in place to actively discourage authors from exercising the rights to their own content.

For this reason, we adopt a completely different approach at Ignite Press. After we have published and launched a client's book, we provide our client with all the files associated with their book. We send them the interior layout files along with the Kindle/ebook files. We send them the layered cover artwork so it can be easily edited if needed. We even send a list of logins for all accounts where the book is hosted. If we perform a bestseller launch, we also send a thorough launch report and screenshots to document the results. A business coach of mine once told me that we should handle things in entirely the opposite fashion. He told me that we should be like a utility company for our clients. Just like we all have to go through the utility company to get our electricity, he said our publishing clients should have to go through us for everything related to their books—at an expense, of course. Well, that is not how we choose to work.

If you work with us to publish your book and you want to do something else with your content later on, no problem. We provide all your files and logins to facilitate the free exercise of your rights. On the other hand, if you want us to help you on other projects in the future, we stand ready. Ultimately, we only want to work with people who want to work with us. I recommend you look for that kind of treatment wherever you go and whatever you do. No one deserves to have their book held hostage, and everyone deserves the right to take their business where they want. It just makes sense.

What Kind of Publishing is Right for You?

This is often a very easy question to answer. If you have a huge following and brand, and you can afford to wait a year or two to see your book in print, traditional publishing may be a good solution for you. Seek out a publishing agent that specializes in your genre. Just be wary of the tradeoffs that occur in traditional contracts.

If traditional publishing is not a fit for you, you still have two options. If you have more time than money and don't mind problem solving, or if you love to DIY projects, self-publishing may be good for you. It will allow you to have complete control, protect your rights, and proceed with the least expense.

If, however, you have more money than time and would rather work with a professional publisher to create a quality book, hybrid publishing may be the best option. Hybrid publishing will allow you to maintain creative (and legal) control of your content while creating the best possible representation of you and your brand. At the same time, you can take advantage of professional editing and layout, expert cover design, and widespread publishing and distribution, and still get your books at cost using print-on-demand technology. If you are willing to make the investment, hybrid publishing really is the best of both worlds.

Our Offer for You

Would you like to have a brief call with Everett to discuss your book and your publishing options? If you go to IgnitePress.us/meet, you can reserve a complimentary book consultation.

We can discuss:

- What is the target market for your book?
- What do you want your book to accomplish for you?
- What book formats are available (and appropriate)?
- What can you do *right now* to prepare for publishing?
- What should you be doing to pave the way for a bestseller launch?
- What budget should you expect for your launch?
- What other questions do you have?

We can address these questions and others in your complimentary book consultation. Just go to IgnitePress.us/meet and reserve your consultation.

Whatever you do...

Whatever you do and however you choose to do it, write your book. Get it out to the world. The world deserves to hear your message and to learn from your wisdom. Your accumulated knowledge needs to be shared. Whether you decide to publish by yourself or with a hybrid publisher, or if you decide to wade through the challenging waters of traditional publishing, the power of the published awaits you.

ABOUT THE AUTHORS

*C*athy Fyock is The Business Book Strategist, and works with thought leaders and professionals who want to write a book as a business growth strategy. She is the author of ten books, including *On Your Mark: From First Word to First Draft in Six Weeks*, *Blog-2Book: Repurposing Content to Discover the Book You've Already Written*, and *The Speaker Author: Sell More Books and Book More Speeches* (with Lois Creamer). Her book, *Authority*, was a #1 bestseller on Amazon and landed on the *Wall Street Journal* and *USA Today* bestseller lists as well. Since beginning her book coaching business in 2014, she's helped more than 200 professionals become published authors. She believes that authors change the world, one word at a time.

She can be reached at Cathy@CathyFyock.com. Visit her website at CathyFyock.com.

*E*verett O'Keefe is a *Wall Street Journal, USA Today,* and International #1 Bestselling Author. *The Power of the Published* is his most recent solo work. He has also helped create and launch nearly 100 bestselling books for his clients. Everett speaks across the nation on the power of publishing. He is the founder of Ignite Press, a hybrid publishing company that specializes in helping entrepreneurs, as well as business and medical professionals, ignite their businesses by becoming bestselling authors.

Everett is the winner of multiple awards, including the Publish and Profit Award for Excellence in Publishing, the Make Market & Launch It Award for Product Creation, and the Top Gun Consulting Award, among others. He is the co-founder of the Business Accelerator Group, a high-level mastermind group composed of international marketers and publishers. He also founded the Mastermind Retreat and hosts international mastermind events.

In 2019, Everett founded The Book Publishers Network, a group of publishers, publishing consultants, book coaches and other book professionals. In 2020, he founded The Publishers Mastermind in order to help support publishing professionals from around the world.

Everett is sought out as a speaker, coach, and consultant by authors and marketing experts worldwide. With a passion for entrepreneurialism, Everett helps his clients become recognized experts in their fields through speaking and authorship while allowing his clients to focus on their own areas of giftedness.

You can reach Everett through his company's website at https://IgnitePress.us.

Everett can also be found on social media at these sites:
https://www.facebook.com/ignitepress/
https://www.linkedin.com/in/everettokeefe/

RELEVANT BOOKS
BY CATHY FYOCK AND EVERETT O'KEEFE

Cathy's Books:

- *On Your Mark: From First Word to First Draft in Six Weeks*
- *Blog2Book: Repurposing Content to Discover the Book You've Already Written*
- *The Speaker Author: Sell More Books and Book More Speeches*
- *Authority: Strategic Concepts from 15 International Thought Leaders to Create Influence, Credibility and a Competitive Edge for You and Your Business*

Everett's Books:

- *The Power of the Published: How Rapidly Authoring a Book Can Ignite Your Business and Your Life*
- *Books 2 Bucks: The Top 20 Ways to Make Money with Your Book (Even If You Haven't Written it Yet)*
- *Authority: Strategic Concepts from 15 International Thought Leaders to Create Influence, Credibility and a Competitive Edge for You and Your Business*
- *Book Writing Bible: Expert Secrets on How to Write, Sell, & Market Your Book Online*
- *Your Epic Book Launch: How to Write A Book, Launch Your Book into a #1 International Bestseller, Raise Your Income, Make Money Online, and Build a 6 to 7 Figure Business... Even If You Don't Know How*
- *There's Money in This Book: 17 Secrets from a Marketing Mastermind*

MAY WE ASK A FAVOR?

Hey, it's Cathy and Everett here.

We hope you've enjoyed this workbook and have found it to be useful.

Would you consider giving it a rating wherever you bought the book? Online book stores are more likely to promote a book when they feel good about its content, and reader reviews are a great barometer for a book's quality.

So please go to the website of wherever you bought the book, search for our names and the book title, and leave a review. If you're able, perhaps consider adding a picture of you holding the book. That increases the likelihood your review will be accepted!

Many thanks in advance,

Cathy & Everett

WILL YOU SHARE THE LOVE?

Get this book for a friend, associate, or family member!

If you have found this book valuable and know others who would find it useful, consider buying them a copy as a gift. Special bulk discounts are available if you would like your whole team or organization to benefit from reading this. Just contact Cathy@ CathyFyock.com.

**Would You Like Cathy or Everett to
Speak to Your Organization?**

Book Cathy or Everett Now!

Cathy and Everett accept a limited number of speaking engagements each year. To learn how you can bring their message to your organization, call or email:

Cathy Fyock: Cathy@CathyFyock.com
502-445-6539

Everet O'Keefe: IgnitePress.us
559-477-4202

www.ingramcontent.com/pod-product-compliance
Lightning Source LLC
Chambersburg PA
CBHW051759200326
41597CB00025B/4620